CRACKING THE CODE

OF

CONSUMER DESIRE

The Ultimate Guide on How to Make Your Products Irresistible and Achieve $100M Deals

Raymond D. Richeson

TABLE OF CONTENT

INTRODUCTION

The Quest For $100 Million Deals

In the core of a clamoring city, there was a little shop that many neglected, yet for the people who paused for a minute to enter, it held a universe of marvels. Alice, the retailer, was a visionary, and her store, suitably named "Alice's Fantasies," was a domain of eccentricity and charm.

In the early hours of every day, when the sun's most memorable beams painted the city in gold, Alice would open the entryways of her safe-haven. She'd tidy off the racks that held her carefully assembled ponders, each piece imbued with her limitless inventiveness and love. As far as she might be concerned, they were more than objects; they were bits of her heart.

In any case, as she looked at her enchanting manifestations and the sticker prices that enhanced them, Alice couldn't resist the opportunity to contemplate whether her fantasies were excessively aggressive. Her unassuming shop appeared to be a simple firefly in the evening, encompassed by the stunning splendor of corporate goliaths that lingered like high rises around her.

One evening, as the downpour tapped delicately on her shop's window, Alice's eyes loaded up with tears. She murmured to herself, "How might I make them see what I find in these marvels? How might I transform outsiders into adherents, into admirers who figure out the enchantment inside every creation?"

Thus, started the odyssey of a visionary, an excursion through the city's lively roads as well as through the profundities of human craving. Alice's interest was filled by a fantasy that many thoughts about unimaginable, yet it was a fantasy that had caught her heart, a fantasy that would not diminish in spite of the world's questions.

Part 1: Unraveling Customer Wants

The clamoring roads of Virtuoso Valley, where Alice's shop stood, were like veins of a rambling creature. They conveyed individuals from varying backgrounds, each determined by their own cravings and dreams. As we set out on our mission to comprehend the code of customer want, it's fundamental to perceive that each buy, each exchange, is a dance of feelings and necessities, wants and items of common sense.

The Core of Each and every Buy

Each buy, from the littlest knickknack to the most excellent securing, has a close to home heartbeat. A cadence synchronizes with the heartbeat of want. To Alice, her shop was loaded up with something other than objects; it was an assortment of dreams that could be held, contacted, and experienced. As she looked at her manifestations, she realizes that they were vessels of human yearning, transporters of feeling.

Take, for example, the antique music box that she had affectionately reestablished. It wasn't simply an old piece of apparatus; it was wistfulness in a wooden casing. For the ideal individual, it played tunes as well as an ensemble of recollections. The sticker price on it wasn't actually necessary to focus on the expense of materials or work; it was about the worth of those recollections.

Understanding the profound heart of each and every buy is the most vital phase in deciphering the code of purchaser want. It's tied in with understanding that behind each exchange, there's a story, a believing, a craving that drives the choice to purchase. It's tied in with embracing the way that buyers are not simply judicious creatures pursuing legitimate decisions; they are close to home animals, and their cravings are the compass that directs their buying process.

The Close to home Association

Buyer want is well established in feelings, and this association powers the driving force of business. At the point when Alice welcomed her clients, she wasn't only introducing items; she was welcoming them into a universe of marvel and joy. She comprehended that the wizardry of her shop wasn't in the wood and metal of her manifestations;

it was in the grins they brought, the sentimentality they evoked, and the charm they enlivened.

Every client who entered "Alice's Fantasies" was on an individual excursion. They conveyed with them the heaviness of their day, their fantasies, and their recollections. Furthermore, inside her shop, they tracked down a safe-haven — where their cravings could track down articulation.

This profound association isn't restricted to little shops or interesting knickknacks. It's a basic part of each and every purchasing experience. At the point when you purchase some espresso from a nearby bistro, it's not just about caffeine; it's about the fragrance, the solace, the feeling of local area. At the point when you put resources into an extravagance vehicle, it's not just about transportation; it's about esteem, status, and the sensation of force.

Understanding this close to home association is the way to opening the code of buyer want. It's tied in with perceiving that behind each item or administration, there's a chance to take advantage of the hearts and psyches of your clients.

In the parts that follow, we'll dig further into the profound embroidery of purchaser want. We'll investigate the layers of yearning, the shades of feeling, and the ensemble of need that characterize the scene of buying choices. Also, as we do, you'll find how to mesh your items and administrations into this embroidered artwork, making associations that transform outsiders into faithful clients, and dreams into $100 million arrangements.

Part 2: The Scene of Lead Age

As Alice proceeded with her excursion into the universe of customer want, she before long understood that understanding her crowd was central. A sharp feeling of who her potential clients were and how to find and draw in them would establish the groundwork for her journey for 0 million arrangements. This part investigates the scene of lead age, helping you recognize and interface with the right crowd.

Figuring out Your Crowd

Each effective excursion begins considering a reasonable objective. For Alice's situation, that objective was transforming outsiders into ardent admirers of her high-quality marvels. To do this, she needed to comprehend what her listeners might be thinking all around.

The most vital phase in this cycle was making nitty gritty client personas. These imaginary people addressed various fragments of her potential client base. By understanding their necessities, wants, problem areas, and inspirations, Alice could tailor her items, advertising messages, and procedures to resound with every persona.

Client personas permitted Alice to address vital inquiries:

- Who are my optimal clients?

- What is their socioeconomics (age, orientation, area, pay)?

- What is their psychographics (values, interests, way of life)?

- What difficulties do they confront that my items can address?

- What advantages do they look for in my manifestations?

For example, Alice found that a portion of her clients were youthful experts who esteemed extraordinary and practical items. Others were more seasoned authorities who valued sentimentality and the tales behind each piece. Outfitted with this understanding, she could create her promoting efforts and item contributions to engage the two portions.

Finding and Drawing in the Right Leads

Whenever you've characterized your ideal interest group, the subsequent stage is to find and draw in the right leads, the people who resound with your contributions and are bound to become faithful clients. This cycle involves a blend of methodologies and strategies:

i. **Content Promoting:** Making top caliber, enlightening, and connecting with content that requests to your interest group can attract possible clients to your image. This content can take different structures, including blog entries, recordings, online entertainment updates, from there, the sky is the limit. For Alice, it implied sharing tales about the set of experiences and craftsmanship behind her manifestations.

ii. **Website design enhancement (Site improvement):** Advancing your web-based presence to show up unmistakably in web search tool results can assist you with arriving at potential clients effectively searching for what you offer. Alice guaranteed her site was all around improved, making it simpler for those looking for interesting and high-quality things to find her shop.

iii. **Online Entertainment Commitment:** Laying out major areas of strength for a via web-based entertainment stages pertinent to your crowd can be a strong method for interfacing with possible clients. Alice routinely posted pictures of her items on stages like Instagram, making visual stories that resounded with her clients.

iv. **Networking:** Building connections inside your industry and with potential clients is an important strategy. Alice went to neighborhood craftsman markets, where she met similar people who shared her enthusiasm for carefully assembled things.

v. **Reference Projects:** Empowering existing clients to allude loved ones can be a powerful lead age technique. Offering motivators, like limits or select things, can rouse clients to get the message out about your image.

Alice discovered that fruitful lead age was not exclusively about amount but rather additionally about quality. It wasn't just about aggregating leads yet associating with the ideal individuals who genuinely valued her manifestations.

In the parts that follow, we'll jump further into systems for coming to and drawing in with your leads, sustaining those associations, and eventually changing them into dedicated clients. Alice's process was simply starting, and not entirely set in stone to find the way that would lead her to $100 million arrangements.

Part 3: Creating an Appealing Incentive

As Alice proceeded with her journey to open the code of shopper want, she knew that making a compelling incentive was the way to transforming outsiders into excited clients. In this section, we dig into the specialty of making an offer that catches consideration and flashes the craving to draw in with your items or administrations.

Making a Proposition They Can't Help it

The groundwork of an effective undertaking lies in the worth you give to your clients. All in all, how might your items or administrations at any point help them that no other person would be able? This is the pith of your incentive.

For Alice, the offer was established in the pith of her high-quality marvels. She understood that what put her manifestations aside was their actual qualities, yet the accounts, feelings, and recollections they conveyed. She started to create her incentive by resolving key inquiries:

i. What issues do my items or administrations tackle? Alice's manifestations offered a novel answer for clients hoping to communicate their singularity and interface with significant stories.

ii. What advantages do they give? Her hand tailored things offered a profound association, a feeling of wistfulness, and an appreciation for creativity.

iii. What makes them not the same as contenders? Alice's manifestations were not efficiently manufactured; they were individual bits of craftsmanship with a story behind everyone.

Making a charming offer implied plainly conveying these interesting offering focuses to likely clients. Alice understood that her offer was not just about the item; it was about the experience, the inclination, and the recollections that her clients would acquire.

In your own business, it's critical to recognize what separates your items or administrations. Consider:

i. The issues your items or administrations address.

ii. The advantages they give to clients.

iii. How they contrast from the opposition.

These experiences will assist you with making an incentive that resounds with your ideal interest group.

The Sorcery of Significant worth Correspondence

Having areas of strength for a recommendation is just a portion of the fight; the other half lies in successful worth correspondence. Alice comprehended that having a convincing story behind her creations wasn't sufficient; she needed to impart it to the world.

Here are a few techniques for successfully imparting your incentive:

i. **Clear Informing:** Your incentive ought to be brief and straightforward. Clients ought to rapidly get a handle on why your items or administrations are important.

ii. **Drawing in Narrating:** Use narrating to interface genuinely with your crowd. Share the narratives behind your image, items, or administrations. Alice's tales about the craftsman's who made her marvels and the set of experiences behind each piece added a layer of profundity and profound reverberation.

iii. **Visual Allure:** Visual substance, like top notch pictures and recordings, can grandstand your items or administrations in real life. Alice's web-based entertainment posts, exhibiting her manifestations in gorgeous settings, were instrumental in conveying their allure.

iv. **Client Tributes:** Positive criticism from fulfilled clients fills in as strong social evidence. Share client surveys and tributes that feature the worth your contributions convey.

v. **Consistency:** Guarantee that your offer is predictable across all promoting channels and materials. This forms areas of strength for an intelligent brand character.

Key Note:

Alice's process instructed her that the genuine sorcery of significant worth correspondence was in making a profound association between the client and her manifestations. By making a convincing offer and really conveying it, she pulled in additional leads as well as transformed them into clients who couldn't avoid her handmade miracles.

In the parts ahead, we'll investigate more systems to refine your offer, make it significantly really charming, and progress forward with the way toward $100 million arrangements.

Part 4: Building Trust and Believability

As Alice's excursion to change leads into faithful clients proceeded, she perceived the meaning of building trust and validity. This section investigates the fundamental job these components play all the while and how you can ingrain them into your own business to make enduring client connections.

The Foundations of Buyer Trust

Trust is the establishment whereupon client connections are assembled. It's the conviction that your items or administrations will convey as guaranteed, and that the client's general benefits are at the front line of your business. For Alice, trust was the core of her high-quality miracles — clients believed that each piece conveyed a piece of her heart and was made with care and scrupulousness.

Here are a few vital perspectives to consider in building purchaser trust:

i. **Transparency:** Straightforwardness is tied in with being transparent with your clients. Alice made it a highlight share the tales behind her manifestations, the materials utilized, and individuals engaged with creating each piece. Straightforwardness establishes a climate of genuineness and legitimacy.

ii. **Consistency:** Consistency in item quality and client care is fundamental. Clients need to realize they can expect similar degree of greatness each time they cooperate with your business.

iii. **Reliability:** Might your clients at any point rely upon you to convey as guaranteed? For Alice, conveying items on time and it were non-debatable to give brilliant client support. Dependability is a basic part of trust.

iv. **Security:** In a web-based world, security is a main issue. Clients need to believe that their own and monetary data is protected while communicating with your business. Executing secure installment choices and information assurance measures is vital.

v. **Social Verification:** Positive criticism from different clients, as audits and tributes, gives social evidence that your items or administrations merit trusting. Alice effectively urged fulfilled clients to leave surveys, which further approved her image.

In building trust, consistency is vital. By reliably following through on your commitments and showing that you focus on the prosperity and fulfillment of your clients, you make a feeling of trust that runs profound.

Techniques for Building Validity

Believability remains closely connected with trust yet centers around your business' mastery and unwavering quality inside its industry. It's tied in with laying out your image as a believable wellspring of information or arrangements. Alice comprehended that building validity was tied in with showing her ability as a craftsman.

Here are a few techniques to fabricate validity:

i. **Quality and Greatness:** Take a stab at greatness in all that you do. Guarantee that your items or administrations satisfy or surpass industry guidelines. Alice constantly sharpened her specialty, looking to make ponders that were wonderful as well as flawless in quality.

ii. **Thought Authority:** Share your insight and bits of knowledge in your field. Whether through blog entries, studios, or online courses, situating yourself as an idea chief can improve your validity.

iii. **Grants and Acknowledgments**: Assuming your business gets grants or acknowledgments in your industry, show them gladly. Alice was excited when her manifestations got acknowledgment from neighborhood craftsman networks.

iv. **Partnerships:** Working together with legitimate organizations or associations can support your validity. Alice worked with neighborhood noble cause and exhibition halls, which upgraded her standing.

v.   **Client Training:** Teach your clients about your items or administrations. Giving tips, guides, and valuable data exhibits your skill and obligation to assisting your clients with settling on informed decisions.

Key Note:

In Alice's excursion, building believability was not just about demonstrating the worth of her manifestations yet in addition exhibiting her obligation to her specialty and her clients. *Believability was tied in with being perceived as an expert in her field, a brand client could depend on.*

In the sections ahead, we'll dive further into procedures and strategies for building trust and believability, making enduring client connections, and crawling nearer to those $100 million arrangements.

Part 5: Fostering a Triumphant Deals Technique

As Alice's process unfurled, she comprehended that having areas of strength for a procedure was fundamental for transforming leads into fulfilled clients. In this section, we investigate the components of a triumphant deals methodology and how it assumed a significant part in Alice's journey to reach $100 million in deals.

Delineating Your Business Process

An effective deals methodology starts with an unmistakable guide. It's fundamental to comprehend the excursion your clients go through from the second they become mindful of your items or administrations to the second they make a buy. For Alice, this excursion was similar to driving her clients through a mystical story, and her business procedure was the account that directed them.

Here are the critical phases of a deals venture:

i. **Awareness:** This is the stage at which potential clients become mindful of your image or contributions. It's critical to catch their consideration and make a significant initial feeling. For Alice, this frequently started with eye-getting window shows and drawing in web-based entertainment posts that displayed her novel manifestations.

ii. **Interest:** Whenever you've aroused their curiosity, the following stage is to sustain it. Give more data, draw in with their inquiries, and proposition further experiences into what makes your items or administrations unique. Alice facilitated studios and narrating occasions where clients could interface with the accounts behind her carefully assembled ponders.

iii. **Desire:** At this stage, you want to change interest into want. Exhibit the profound and down to earth advantages of your contributions. For Alice, this implied stressing the wistful worth of her manifestations and how they could add magnificence and importance to clients' lives.

iv. **Action:** The last step is to direct clients toward activity, whether it's making a buy, pursuing a help, or making some other wanted move. Clear suggestions to take action, for example, "Purchase Presently" fastens and restricted time offers, can urge clients to make that stride.

Understanding this deals venture and making a brilliant course of action for each stage empowers you to direct possible clients along the way from starting attention to a fruitful buy.

Compelling Procedures for Changing over Leads

To actually change over leads into clients, Alice sharpened her deals procedures. Her methodology was based on a mix of imaginativeness, narrating, and figuring out the extraordinary longings of every client. Here are a few viable deals strategies she utilized:

i.   **Undivided attention:** Give close consideration to what potential clients say, both verbally and non-verbally. This permits you to appropriately figure out their requirements and designer your pitch.

ii. **Consultative Selling:** As opposed to promoting items onto clients, adopt a consultative strategy. Clarify some pressing issues, figure out their objectives, and propose items or administrations that line up with their requirements.

iii. **Storytelling:** Alice's enchanted lay in her capacity to share stories. She laid out pictures with words, depicting the set of experiences and feelings behind each piece. This made the buy more significant as well as made areas of strength for a with clients.

iv. **Desperation and Shortage:** Restricted time offers or elite items can make a need to get moving and urge clients to go with a choice.

v. **Follow-up:** Try not to misjudge the force of follow-up. Numerous deals are shut through determined follow-down and sustaining of the client relationship.

Part 6: The Craft of Sustaining Leads

As Alice's excursion to change leads into gave clients proceeded, she found the meaning of lead sustaining. In this section, we look at the specialty of supporting leads, cultivating connections, and directing possible clients toward becoming steadfast benefactors.

Taking care of the Fire of Want

Lead supporting is the most common way of developing and building associations with leads over the long haul. It's like watching out for a nursery; you plant the seeds, water them, and guarantee they get satisfactory daylight. In Alice's reality, lead sustaining was tied in with stirring up want that at first carried possible clients to her shop.

Here are fundamental components of successful lead supporting:

Personalization: Treat your leads as people. Comprehend their novel requirements and wants and designer your collaborations appropriately. Alice recollected the names and inclinations of her recurrent clients, making a feeling of unique interaction.

i. **Predictable Correspondence:** Push the discussion along. Customary messages, pamphlets, or online entertainment updates can aid you with remaining top-of-mind with your leads. For Alice, this implied sharing stories, sneak looks of new manifestations, and data about impending occasions.

ii. **Esteem Added Content**: Give content that enhances your leads' information or lives. Whether it's the way to guides, blog entries, or industry experiences, Alice guaranteed that her interchanges enhanced her leads.

iii. **Commitment Potential open doors:** Set out open doors for prompts cooperate with your image. Whether it's answering inquiries, going to occasions, or taking part in overviews, commitment cultivates a feeling of association.

iv. **Lead Scoring:** Not all leads are equivalent. Use lead scoring to recognize which leads are bound to as needs be converted and focus on your endeavors.

Alice perceived the worth of long haul leads who had communicated with her image on various occasions.

By supporting leads, you keep them connected with and put resources into your image, improving the probability that they will ultimately become steadfast clients.

The Way to Enduring Connections

Lead sustaining is something beyond a necessary evil; it's tied in with building enduring connections. Alice's process was a demonstration of the force of connections based on trust, common regard, and shared values.

Here are a few techniques to support leads and make enduring connections:

Tuning in and Answering: Effectively pay attention to your leads' criticism and concerns. Answer expeditiously and truly. Alice made it a highlight address client requests and ideas instantly, showing that she esteemed their feedback.

Shock and Enjoyment: Exceed all expectations to shock and joy your leads. Alice infrequently sent written by hand cards to say thanks and little gifts to her most drawn in leads, making snapshots of satisfaction and appreciation.

Instruct and Motivate: Proceed to instruct and rouse your leads. Share experiences, examples of overcoming adversity, and information that lines up with their inclinations and requirements.

i. **Unwaveringness Projects:** Consider unwaveringness projects or select contributions for rehash clients. Alice offered unwaveringness prizes for her continuous clients, which energized recurrent business as well as caused them to feel esteemed.

ii. **Criticism Circle:** Urge prompts give input and utilize their bits of knowledge to work on your items or administrations. Paying attention to their ideas and making changes in view of their feedback exhibits your obligation agreeable to them.

Key Note:

In Alice's excursion, lead supporting wasn't just about deals; it was tied in with making a local area of faithful benefactors who treasured her manifestations. Whether you're occupied with handmade marvels, innovation arrangements, or some other item or administration, sustaining leads and building enduring connections is the way to $100 million in bargains.

In the parts to come, we'll investigate methodologies to scale your tasks, arrange and close high-stakes arrangements, and draw motivation from certifiable examples of overcoming adversity. The excursion proceeds, and the objective is reachable.

Part 7: Scaling for $100 Million Arrangements

Alice's process had been one of self-revelation and development. She had changed her modest shop into a flourishing business, at this point she actually sought to arrive at the terrific objective of $100 million in bargains. In this section, we investigate systems for scaling your tasks, extending your range, and getting ready for those high-stakes bargains.

Growing Your Scope and Desires

Scaling your business is tied in with arriving at new levels while keeping up with the pith that makes it one of a kind. It's a sensitive harmony among development and protecting the qualities and characteristics that put you aside. For Alice, this excursion implied growing her shop past the limits of Virtuoso Valley.

Here are a few techniques for growing your span and desires:

i. **Statistical surveying:** See new business sectors and socioeconomics that could profit from your items or administrations. Alice led exploration to distinguish close by urban communities and districts with a craving for one of a kind high quality thing.

ii. **Diversification:** Consider growing your item or administration contributions. Alice presented new lines of high-quality marvels, taking care of a more extensive scope of client interests.

iii. **E-commerce:** Assuming your business is fundamentally physical, investigate the universe of online business. Alice laid out an internet-based store, permitting her to contact a worldwide crowd.

iv. **Diversifying and Associations:** Cooperate with different organizations or consider diversifying your idea. Alice investigated organizations with neighborhood craftsman and displays to broaden her scope.

v. **Put resources into Showcasing:** As you scale, distribute assets for showcasing and promoting to contact a bigger crowd. Alice's showcasing financial plan expanded as her business extended.

Growing your scope is tied in with embracing new skylines, going ahead with reasonable plans of action, and guaranteeing that your business is prepared to serve a more extensive crowd.

Saddling Innovation for Development

In the present computerized age, innovation can be an incredible asset for scaling your business. Whether it's computerizing processes, further developing client cooperation, or growing your web-based presence, innovation can assume a fundamental part in accomplishing your objectives.

i. **Client Relationship The executives (CRM):** Execute a CRM framework to oversee and dissect client information. Alice utilized a CRM to follow client communications, buy history, and inclinations, permitting her to customize her contributions.

ii. **Internet business Stages:** Assuming you're growing on the web, pick a powerful web-based business stage. Alice's internet-based store was based on an easy to use stage that worked with exchanges and gave clients a consistent shopping experience.

iii. **Web-based Entertainment and Internet Promoting:** Influence virtual entertainment and web-based promoting to contact a more extensive crowd. Alice utilized designated advertisements via virtual entertainment to draw in clients who lined up with her image.

iv. **Information Examination:** Use information investigation to acquire experiences into client conduct and patterns. Alice routinely examined information to arrive at informed conclusions about her product offerings and promoting methodologies.

Innovation can be a significant accomplice in your scaling process, permitting you to arrive at additional clients, offer a superior client experience, and smooth out tasks.

Staying Consistent with Your Quintessence

As you scale your tasks, staying consistent with the quintessence of your business is essential. Alice never neglected to focus on her enthusiasm for high quality marvels and the narratives they told. It was this genuineness that kept on resounding with her clients as she extended.

In the sections ahead, we'll dig into the craft of exchange and the procedures for shutting high-stakes bargains. The way to $100 million in bargains is cleared sincerely, development, and a promise to your exceptional quintessence.

Part 8: Arranging and Shutting High-Stakes Arrangements

The stupendous objective of $100 million arrangements was not too far off for Alice. Nonetheless, to arrive at it, she expected to become the best at discussion and the methodologies for shutting high-stakes bargains. In this part, we investigate the methods and rules that directed her towards progress.

The Dance of Discussion

Discussion is a sensitive dance — a compromise where the two players mean to track down a commonly valuable understanding. Alice wound up in this dance commonly, whether it was with discount purchasers, expected accomplices, or gatherers searching for uncommon pieces.

Here are the critical components of fruitful discussion:

i. **Know Your Worth:** Comprehend the worth of what you offer that might be of some value. For Alice, it was the uniqueness and profound association of her manifestations. Realizing your worth assists you with haggling from a place of solidarity.

ii. **Undivided attention:** Listen cautiously to the next party's necessities, wants, and concerns. This not just permits you to address their focuses actually yet in addition exhibits regard and compassion.

iii. **Mutual benefit Outlook:** Move toward discussions with a mutually beneficial mentality. Look for arrangements that benefit the two players. Alice accepted that each arrangement ought to leave the two sides feeling fulfilled and energized.

iv. **Tolerance and Steadiness:** Exchange can take time, and in some cases, it requires diligence. Alice didn't race into bargains yet endured in her endeavors to find arrangements that lined up with her qualities and objectives.

v. **Flexibility:** Be available to think twice about adjust to evolving conditions. Alice was ready to change terms or make concessions when it was to the greatest advantage of an arrangement.

Effective exchange is tied in with figuring out something worth agreeing on and building positive, enduring associations with those you work with.

Methodologies for Shutting High-Stakes Arrangements

With regards to shutting high-stakes bargains, a few methodologies can fundamentally upgrade your odds of coming out on top:

i. **Get ready Completely:** Information is power. Research the other party, their requirements, and their set of experiences. This arrangement permits you to enter discussions with certainty and knowledge.

ii. **Fabricate Connections:** Well before high-stakes exchanges start, concentrate on building associations with key chiefs. Trust and compatibility can be strong resources in shutting serious deals.

iii. **Explain Your Targets:** Characterize your goals and wanted results plainly. Having an exact vision of what you need to accomplish assists you with keeping on track during dealings.

iv. **Influence Your Incentive:** Feature what makes your items or administrations exceptional and fundamental. Alice stressed the close to home association her hand tailored ponders offered, making them overpowering to authorities and lovers.

v. **Arrange Gradually:** Think about separating enormous arrangements into more modest, reasonable stages. This can make dealings less scary and make a progression of wins that form trust.

vi. **Incorporate Legitimate Direction:** For high-stakes gives, it's wise to include lawful advice to guarantee that arrangements are impermeable and give assurance to the two players.

vii. **Observe Achievement:** At the point when a high-stakes bargain is shut, commend the accomplishment with your group. It recognizes their diligent effort as well as constructs a feeling of achievement and inspiration for future undertakings.

Key Note:

As Alice explored the universe of high-stakes bargains, she found that outcome in dealings was not exclusively about winning; it was tied in with encouraging trust and setting out open doors for enduring organizations.

In the parts to come, we'll investigate true examples of overcoming adversity and gain experiences from the people who have accomplished the sought after $100 million arrangements. The excursion proceeds, and the objective is reachable.

Part 9: Gaining from Examples of overcoming adversity

As Alice moved toward her objective of $100 million in bargains, she perceived the benefit of gaining from the people who had previously made progress. In this section, we investigate certifiable examples of overcoming adversity and gain experiences from people and organizations that have achieved exceptional arrangements and transformed the business world.

Wins and Bits of knowledge

The excursion to progress is frequently cleared with the tales of those who've preceded us. Alice had faith in the force of gaining from the victories of others, and she anxiously looked for motivation from organizations and people who had accomplished surprising arrangements.

The following are a couple of key examples of overcoming adversity that Alice revealed on her mission:

i. **The Tech Trend-setter:** One example of overcoming adversity highlighted a tech trailblazer who changed a little startup into a tech goliath. Alice was motivated by the pioneer's devotion to their vision, their eagerness to proceed with potentially dangerous courses of action, and their capacity to adjust to the consistently changing tech scene.

ii. **The Craftsman Aggregate:** Another moving story was that of a craftsman aggregate that had laid out a worldwide presence. Alice was attracted to their obligation to saving the substance of hand tailored creativity while growing their arrive at through organizations and internet business.

iii. **The Specialty Advertiser:** A specialty advertiser had cut out a remarkable space in a serious market. Alice was intrigued by their capacity to recognize an undiscovered market and designer their items and promoting to take care of a particular and faithful crowd.

These examples of overcoming adversity gave significant experiences and illustrations:

i. **Vision and Versatility:** Fruitful people and organizations have an unmistakable vision, but at the same time they're versatile. They turn when essential and embrace change as a feature of development.

ii. **Versatility and Hazard Taking:** Accomplishing astounding arrangements frequently includes flexibility notwithstanding challenges and reasonable plans of action taking. Achievement is seldom a straight way, and mishaps are important for the excursion.

iii. **Client Driven Approach:** Putting the client at the focal point of each and every choice is a typical characteristic among fruitful organizations. About understanding client needs and creating arrangements meet them.

iv. **Local area and Cooperation:** Numerous examples of overcoming adversity included coordinated effort and building networks around their image. Alice saw that organizations that encouraged a feeling of having a place and imparted values to their clients frequently flourished.

These examples of overcoming adversity filled in as inspiration for Alice and built up her conviction that accomplishing $100 million in bargains was feasible with the right blend of vision, versatility, and client driven systems.

Key Note:

Alice's process was not even close to finished, yet she was currently outfitted with motivation and experiences from the individuals who had strolled the way to progress. In the sections that follow, we'll investigate the finish of her mission, from want to dedication and the acknowledgment of dreams.

CONCLUSION

Alice's excursion to decipher the code of customer want and change leads into $100 million arrangements was a mind-blowing odyssey loaded up with learning, development, and motivation. Her story fills in as a demonstration of the force of vision, strength, and resolute obligation to one's enthusiasm and values.

In the pages of this book, we've investigated the different sections of her astounding excursion:

- We started with the flash of want, an enthusiasm to make and impart hand tailored marvels to the world. It was the craving to transform outsiders into admirers and clients into enthusiasts.

- Through the sections that followed, we dove into the scene of lead age, creating appealing incentives, building trust and validity, and the craft of sustaining leads. We revealed the methodologies and strategies that lay the foundation for effective business attempts.

- We then wandered into the domain of scaling for $100 million arrangements, growing reach and embracing innovation while remaining consistent with one's substance. The excursion of development and extension was set apart by advancement and the conservation of the extraordinary characteristics that put Alice aside.

- The specialty of discussion and shutting high-stakes bargains turned into the following objective, where we investigated the subtleties of exchange, the significance of shared benefit, and the procedures for accomplishing aggressive arrangements.

- In Section 9, we gained from certifiable examples of overcoming adversity, drawing bits of knowledge and motivation from organizations and people who had accomplished astounding arrangements. Their accounts supported the significance of vision, flexibility, strength, and a client driven approach.

As we arrive at the finish of Alice's excursion, we track down her remaining on the cusp of her fantasy. She has acquired information and experience as well as a profound appreciation for the specialty of business and the worth of veritable associations with clients.

Alice's journey to reach $100 million in bargains is a demonstration of the way that with energy, reason, and the right systems, striking dreams can become reality. Her process has motivated us to embrace our longings, sustain them with care, and seek after our objectives with immovable dedication.

The way to acknowledging dreams is generally difficult, yet it is dependably worth the effort. As you set out on your own excursion, may Alice's story act as a directing light, enlightening the way to your own yearnings and the acknowledgment of your novel cravings. Whether in the realm of high-quality miracles, innovation, or some other field, recollect that the way to progress is fabricated slowly but surely, with every section driving you nearer to the terrific finale of your own noteworthy story.